Take Care of the Children in Your Own Backyard

Earline Carr

Order this book online at www.trafford.com
or email orders@trafford.com

Most Trafford titles are also available at major online book retailers.

© Copyright 2011 Earline Carr.

All rights reserved. No part of this publication may be reproduced, stored in a retrieval system, or transmitted, in any form or by any means, electronic, mechanical, photocopying, recording, or otherwise, without the written prior permission of the author.

Printed in the United States of America.

ISBN: 978-1-4269-9443-2

Library of Congress Control Number: 2011916496

Trafford rev. 09/15/2011

 www.trafford.com

North America & international
toll-free: 1 888 232 4444 (USA & Canada)
phone: 250 383 6864 ♦ fax: 812 355 4082

Take Care of the children in your own backyard

Earline Carr

Dedication

This book is dedicated to my family.
Also to New Home BC
Pastor and Mrs. Robert C. Blakes

A special thanks to
Ms. Ruby Lockhart
and a to a fellow author
Ms. Pamela Reed

Contents

Preface v
Introduction vi
Drugs 1
Mothers 11
Fathers 30
Young Ladies 38
Afterward 50

PREFACE

In this Katrina flooded city, and surrounding parishes, plus the oil spill, gone from a "chocolate city" where murder has become something of the "norm."

Some people will be angry with me for stating the truth. But this is a fact, black on black crime every night and sometimes in broad daylight. Innocent blood has been and still being shed in the city.

Jail houses are filled with small time crooks as well as blue collar, and white collar criminals. What is going to become of New Orleans and our culture? Where will I get those fresh shrimp, and crabs to make gumbo. Should we allow the "few" who could care less about New Orleans to win.

I say, NO! We must fight to keep and make this city a place to draw people to it, not flee from it.

GOD HELP US

Introduction

Shock

- The six am news reported that someone killed five people in one home while robbing them of money to support his heroin habit.

- Before noon that same day, someone punched a sixty year old woman in the face and snatched her purse. Why? To buy some crack.

- Turf Wars, caused by people who do not own any **TURF.**

- What is wrong when a kid goes to school everyday for twelve years, and Johnny cannot read?

- Women allowing men to move-in their homes, over their children, and later learns that he is a sex offender.

- After looking at what is going on in the world today, I decided to write this book. I am hoping to bring awareness to parents and others that they can make a difference in their families.

Drugs

Is this your son?

We are so afraid for you

Your children are watching you

I Love you, Son

Working at a fast food place is better than selling crack

We watch you smoke the crack pipe

Children do not always do what you say do, but they will imitate what they see you do.
Is this where your teens learn how to use the crack pipe to get high? Your children and their friends have seen you scoring dope.

You were such a "good" role mode. These are a few of the people who followed your lead.
- Your son gets his high sticking **heroin** into his veins.
- Your two daughters decided **crack** was the way to go.

SEE, you turned out to be a role model, after all.

Trail Mix

Parents this is another trend to watch out for. If you have any leftover sleeping pills, muscle relaxers, please flush them. Do not leave them in the medicine cabinet or bedside table.

Trail Mix Party

The word is out, there will be a trail mix party. To attend, you must steal at least two pills from your parents medicine cabinet. Not just any pill, it has to be something that can make a person high. Pills left over from a tooth extraction, or back ache, or sleeping pills.

To get the party started, all pills are thrown into a hat and shaken up. Everyone reaches in and takes a pill, gets a drink and wait for the high to kick in. **WHO THOUGHT OF THIS KILLER IDEA.** After getting high, everyone picks someone they will have sex with. Now lets see, after the party is over. Who did you have sex with? Did you have sex with more than one person?

If you become pregnant, do you wonder which one impregnated you? Which guy you had sex with gave you HIV?

Did anyone give this a second thought before attending the party? Who in their right mind would take a pill from a hat, not knowing the strength of the pills, nor the side effects.

After you have done all the pill popping and having sex with Tom, Dick and Harry.

The questions asked here are the questions you should have asked yourself before attending the party.

Crystal Methamphetamine

Crystal Meth is related to cocaine, but it is much more toxic. Meth is made from battery acid, kerosene, anti-freeze, iodine, red devil lye, Hydrochloric Acid, and drain cleaner. Just to name a few.

Would you sit down at the table and eat a spoon of drain cleaner, a spoon of lye, mixed with Hydrochloric acid. I guess you would say no. But why would you mix-up these ingredients and shoot it into your veins?

Meth destroys the area of the brain that process emotion and mood. The results are delusion, uncontrolled anger, among other things.

According to officials once a person builds up a tolerance for meth, he or she will desire more and more meth.

Some user's go without food and sleep while indulging in a form of, **BINGING.**

Binging

Binging also known as a **"RUN"** is injecting as much as a gram of meth, every two or three hours over a several day period. They usually continue this until they run out of the drug, or they are to high to continue.

By this time the person could be a full blown addict. A person who uses meth never gets as big a high as he or she did the first time.

So their time is spent chasing that big high they got the first time.

Chasing this dream leads them to taking more drugs, which sometimes lead to over dose.

Some of the side affects of using <u>Meth</u>amphetamine

- Increased heart rate
- Blurred vision
- Nausea
- Insomnia
- Increased blood pressure
- Chronic Depression
- Distorted thinking
- Convulsions and Tremors
- Permanent nerve damage
- Meth-Mouth (teeth deterioration)

Meth and the environment

Due to the ease to obtain the chemicals to make the drugs. For years in homes or outside sheds using highly poisonous substances, such as lye, sulfuric acid. When they are done they pour those chemicals on the ground, sometimes near a body of water. Bad for the environment.

The Shake and Bake Meth Lab
They've gone mobile

This method came to the attention of some law enforcement in 1999 in some cities, and the year 2000 in others.

Some people claim the process is even more dangerous than the old make shift meth labs. Its also known as the **"One Stop Pot Method."** This method, is produced in a two liter soda bottle. The maker can get a few hits, before having to make another batch.

Everything needed to make this brew can be carried in a back pack. All that is required is a large quantity of over the counter pills, decongestants, allergy and cold remedies. And its shake and bake time.

If this is done while riding in a car, all empties can be thrown out the window while riding. As if we do not have enough to worry about, already.

This mobile method is a extremely dangerous method. If the bottle is shaken the wrong way, or oxygen gets inside, or the cap is loosened to quickly, the bottle has been known to explode into a giant fireball. It's bad enough that you have chosen to be a meth user, but what about the innocent people on the school bus sitting next to you at the red light. Or the pregnant mother on the other side of you. When all of a sudden you loosen the cap to fast, the bottle explodes into a fireball.

Well if you must kill yourself, why not pull over to the side of the road or an empty parking lot. Shake and bake, get your high on, and discord your empties into the nearest dumpster.

Live and Let Live

Mojo or Spice

Something else for parents to look out for. There are several kinds of mojo or spice.
Trance is just one of them, These spices were meant to give off a sweet fragrance, to cover up bad odors. Some people are rolling these herbs in weed papers and smoking it.

Its also been reported that these herbs do not show up on drug test, in some people. User's say the high is more potent than marijuana. Some people reported that using mojo in this way leaves them with the shakes. Others are left with a headache, after the high.

Mojo or Spice is being smoked right in your home, right under your nose. And you think they are burning incense.

Mothers

Role Model

OH! That looks like my Mom.

My mother is showing me the way I should act when I grow up. Maybe I should let my children SEE what I do with my boyfriend, too. When my sister and I go to school, we can tell all our friends what we saw our mom do with her boyfriend.

Here is an idea, when we have "Show and Tell" I can show the class some of the things my mother does with her boyfriend. My sister who is older than I, can act this out with her boyfriend. They do this all the time.

My mother is such a GOOD role model,
Just trying to make a point
Get it

Ladies use Wisdom

Ladies if you are a Section 8 participant and have been provided housing for you and your children, then you need to read this.

STOP! Bringing these men into your house to have sex with you.

So many women are losing their vouchers, which was meant to be a stepping stone to getting their homes. Perhaps, you allow him to live with you, he doesn't have steady income but he does sell drugs from your house. The word gets out, he gets caught.

The incident is reported to the housing agency and you lose your voucher. Now you are headed back to mom's house, with four children. No one is going to feel sorry for you. You brought this on yourself. Think about it, was he worth you losing your house? He has probably moved on to his next victim. You have the power to stop being used! If that man is truly interested in you, he will respect you and desire to help in anyway.

Do Not get caught up in the cycle of being **USED.**

Please tell someone
Sex Offender

Some children do not get the chance to be bad. Also, some do not get a chance to have a normal childhood. Why! Because every night they have to worry about a grown-up coming into their bed room forcing them to have sex.

Some children are extremely frighten because they have been threaten, that if they tell anybody the offender, will hurt or kill their parents.

Parents pay close attention to your children and you will know when something is wrong. Mother's "read" your children the same way you "read" your man. You know when something is not right. Some children behavior will change because they can not say what is bothering them.

They want you to ask them, what is wrong.

Children, please tell someone. Tell a teacher, school counselor, doctor, nurse, your best friend who ever you trust. This abuse can be **STOPPED**, if you expose it!

YOU ARE NOT ALONE

What are you allowing in your home
Stolen items

Parents, please stop allowing your children to bring stolen items into your home. You know, what I am talking about. If you, or a family member did not buy those shoes or video games, then they should not be allowed into your home.

Remember-you are just as guilty as they are for receiving stolen goods into your home.

When you allow the little things to come in, the child thinks it is alright with you. Next, they start bringing in bigger things, such as, computer, wide screen televisions.

Parents, you have enough to worry about just trying to raise them, keeping a roof over their heads, food on the table and dealing with their attitudes.

What are you allowing
stolen items

Do not fall for that old line. Mom, you do not respect my privacy. Privacy and respect has to be earned.

If drugs or stolen items are found in your house, that could bring the entire house down. Some young people do not think things through, so it is up to us, as parents to protect the child and your home. I am sure you would not want the wrong element kicking down your door looking for drugs and money.

Also, the state could take your other children from you for putting them in harms way.

Do not allow your child's "lack of wisdom" to destroy the home.

Neglect
Parents neglect

Its the good old summer time, and it's dark outside. Do you know where your children are? How could you be at peace? Inside the house, when you do not know where your children are.

Shame on you Mom
Its nine thirty pm and your grade school children are still not safe inside the house. Crime and violence happening all around you, and you are still on the phone, making your connections. After all, you have to go to the club tonight. When you here the gunfire, then you want to run outside, screaming where are my children? You can not look for them right now because there is too much shooting outside. After everything settles down, it is now about ten thirty pm.

Your children are brought home by the Police. You act like you're relieved. Your children are safe.

The Police warn you about your children being outside late. After about an hour you manage to forget about the incident, you make your connections and you're off to the club.
I wonder if your children went back outside after you left.

About leaving children in a hot car
I will not judge you

But I would like to speak for the children who can't speak for themselves.
Ask yourself these three questions before you leave a kid in a **hot** car.

- If I leave my children in a hot car will they die before I get back to them.
- But I left the motor running. I did not know the car would kill.
- Will I lose my other children, if I leave my baby in the hot car? **YES!** They will terminate your parental rights and you will go to jail.

Deadbeat Moms

Well, I happen to know a few deadbeat moms, What makes you think you should not pay child support, if you give your children over to your husband or to the system? When a deadbeat mom does not want the responsibility of her, children the father becomes the custodial parent. We all know that the non-custodial gets visitation and pays child support.

Another deadbeat mom, gave her children to their father. She met a new man and had two children for him. When she had to appear in court and have her case heard, she stated to the judge that she should not pay child support to her first children.

Ladies, if you give all the responsibility to the other parent you have to pay.
Sometimes you will pay more than money. Children like that who grow up without you in the household, wonder if they did something wrong or that you left because you did not love them.

You should be prepared to answer the following questions.
- Did we do something wrong?
- Did you ever care about us?
- Do you love your other children, and not us?
- Do you hate us?

Just to name a few. I bet if you were not with the father of the new children, and you had the day to day responsibility of caring for these children, you would want child support, too.

I sincerely hope you are doing the "right" thing for all your children.

Rights!
Should parents read their children email and text messages?

Yes, they should

Your children have the **right** to have a computer in their room, which they do not have to share. They have a **right** to keep their bedroom door closed while doing homework with the opposite sex. They have the **right** to burn incense in their room, when you know they are rolling the incense in weed paper and smoking it. Its called Mojo.

Do you watch the talk shows? As the children get older, they want more **rights**. The **right** to get high at home and they want you to buy the drugs for them. The **right** to have a boyfriend or girlfriend sleepover. Some kids have the **right** to have a lock on their bedroom door, and you do not have the **right** to go in that room. Now parents, do you understand all of these **rights** you have given your children?

Rights-1

Parents Rights!

Parents, these are your **rights**. You have the **right** to put your computer in a public area in your home. The same **right** is extended to you concerning their cell phone. If you pay the bill, and you suspect nude pictures are being sent, get a copy of the text messages. You have that **right**.

If homework is getting done by a group of people or by two people, the bedroom is off limits.

Take back your respect as a parent. You are the good parent that has the **right** to love your children and provide food, clothing, shelter and give them the best education you can afford.

Rights--2

You also have a **right** to search and clean their bedroom. No child should ever have the **right** to stand up to you and say, "Stay out of my room!" When your child needs that kind of privacy, it is time for them to get his/her own apartment.

Please don't misunderstand, we discipline our children in love and not abuse. But our children must understand that we have the **authoritative right** to govern our home, according to what we know is **right.**

If we could safely get our children through adolescent, they will thank us later.

Taking Responsibility for our kids
Kids are like a piece of pottery clay, you have to mold and shape the bowl, before the clay hardens.

The same for a child, you must guide and instill in that child the right things to do. Parents you are that child's first teacher. You must take part in shaping and molding your child/children life before they "harden."

Some teachers have said that they have spent the whole class period trying to get order, so that they can teach. Discipline is not always spanking, but you must get their attention before you can teach them. When a child misbehaves, they should know when they have done something wrong. Do not look the other way. If you happen to be on a phone, put the phone down and tend to your child needs.

If you teach your child discipline at a very early age, and if they don't reject it, it is beneficial to the child and to society.

The bible says in Proverbs chapter-22 verse-6
To train up a child in the way he should go and when he is old, he will not depart from it.

Monitor what your children are watching in the Media

Children are like a "sponge" they soak up everything good and bad. They may not understand everything they see, but their vision is taking it all in.

Televisions can be a productive tool. We have to monitor very closely what our children are watching.

Parents there are cartoons, where cursing and sexual acts are performed. Children are so impressionable. Do not allow them to think that this is what they should be doing at their young age.

Stay alert to what is happening through the media.
The watch word is, **Monitor**

Sleepover

Why do you need to allow your kids to spend the night out? We are living in a day when some people can be evil. Sexual Predators are all around us. There are times when it is not safe to allow your kids to spend the night at a relative's house.

Protect your children as much as possible and do not worry about what people will say. Let them say that you are over protective, you do what is right.

The children will not understand why they can not participate in the sleepover. One of my daughters were invited to a sleepover at her teacher's house. My daughter tried to convince me that I would not have to worry about anything bad happening. She said, "My teacher is very trustworthy." Of course, when I had to tell her no, she was very disappointed.

My daughter was thirteen at that time and she did not understand how it was all right for me to trust her teacher to teach her, but not trust her to be a protector during the sleepover. I explained to her that it was not her teacher I was worried about, it was the other people living in her house.

Everyone in the house may not be as honest as your teacher. It is my job as a parent to protect my children.

I wanted my daughter to know there are other ways to bond with your friends. Some of the ways are:

- Have all night conference calls, each from their home.
- Quick cam with speakers allows you to see and talk to each over the computer.
- Come over on Saturday morning with one of your relatives, or maybe your mom.

I told my daughter, "When you get to be a parent, you will understand."

Wisdom

I am a mother of four children, a foster parent for twenty years. It was my intention to help some children, but while fostering some, I noticed some differences.

It is my opinion that some children, no matter who or where they come from they will succeed. There are others, no matter what you do for them, they will succeed in doing nothing positive.

Once I was asked to take care of a five year old girl. I thought, "This is good, because a lot of bad habits have not been formed." Boy, was I wrong, she imitated everything she learned from her family home. She performed vulgar dances with a smile on her face. This child did not know how to recite the Our Father Prayer, but she knew how to "Drop it like its hot."

On the other side of the coin, is another five year old, who knows nothing but how to be a kid. This child is absorbing the good qualities of good loving parents that helps him or her to excel in life.

A lot of what children learn, come by way of the parents, we take credit when they are good, but we must take some of the responsibility when they perform badly.

If a child is raised up with love, he or she learns to love himself and others. If the child thinks his parents do not care he will not "show" compassion for others. An unloved, uncared for child is like a raw piece of meat. The "**dogs**" on the streets can eat him/her alive or kill them dead.

Mothers remember, the "**pimp**" does not mind teaching your daughters what you did not, plus a few more new TRICKS.

And the Question is
What can we do about the parent that does not know how to parent their children?

This is a suggestion:

There are no quick fixes. It took years for some parents dropping the ball, and letting their children do what they wanted to do. We, parents, did not want to make waves, but we soon found out that we can not be their friend and parent too.

Some years ago, I was helping a nineteen year old pregnant girl. She went to the welfare department for assistance. She was told during the last six months of her pregnancy, that she would be allowed to attend classes for eight hours a day five days a week. In these classes you were taught resume writing, parenting skills, vocabulary, interview skills and how to work/act in an office setting. If they missed a day from the class, their welfare check would be cut accordingly. The program ends when the mother has the baby and get a job.

My suggestion

If this program could have continued for three to five years, we would see more mothers completing courses to better their life style. For example, girls that completed high school would be allowed to get a student loan. There are trades that can help them to become productive tax paying citizens.

Now that is a start in the right direction.

By the way, to those who missed it, I did not say another "give away" program, or something for nothing. I said, **"Student Loan."** Not looking for a hand out; but looking for a way out.

Fathers

Fathers
As seen through the eyes of a child

Have you ever noticed your son staring at you? He does not understand why you can not see that he wants to be with you. Sometimes, your child may "act out" because he needs and wants your attention. He does not know how to express himself or his needs, but he thinks that you do not love him. Nevertheless, when ever you go somewhere dad, he wants to follow.

Have you noticed your routine? When you come home from work, you see your son, rub his head and say, "Hey man," next, you say a few words to his mother and you are on the phone. You are talking to your friends about football and making plans to go to the game. Your son can hear that he is not included in your plans.

The son becomes very angry because dad does not spend time with him. He wants to go to the football game, too. But, dad would not take him because dad wants to go drinking with his friends, after the game.

As seen through the eyes of a child
The child thinks, "I wonder if he knows how old I am or what grade I am in. I just want to scream sometimes and say, Dad! Look at me, I am over here. I love you and want to spend time with you.

Where are you, Dad?

Please don't kick me to the curb like the football

I Want a Bachelor Pad
To: The Men

You have been married for several years with children but you have decided you no longer want to be married. Your tell your wife you want to be free and move out as soon as possible.

Now back to the single life. You have your apartment and you are having your first bachelor party. Your friends are there and you're partying like a twenty year old, WOW! Dad. Does this mean you will never want your family again? OH! Does the thought of "Who is the new man in your house with your three daughter?" ever cross your mind. Are your girls safe?
Remember-you left them UNPROTECTED.

Your ex-wife is vulnerable and she does not know this man as well as she knew you. She does not know his back ground. Your ex-wife feels that she needs to get "her grove back" after you kicked her to the curb.

The new man is sleeping over but she does not know he is a sex offender.

Bachelor Pad

Who knows, after he sleeps with your ex, he might sleep with your daughters. Dad, the one who suffers the most are the children.

I hope this will get the attention of some dads and maybe you will think "twice" before you leave your family unprotected.

Deadbeat Dads
The Cost of Crack

Is it true you have four children?
Do you know that school opens in August or September, every year?
Are you aware that some stores have back to school sales on uniforms and school supplies?

Where are you? Are you "that" busy?

- You were seen with the neighborhood crack dealer at 9:30am. You paid eighty-dollars for breakfast crack.
- Later you went back for brunch crack, and paid eighty-dollars.
- Eighty-dollars more for bedtime crack.
- And do not forget snack crack, in the wee hours

This is what your habit looks like to others.
Cont.

This is what your habit looks like to others.
At $80. dollars a pop, four pops a day, equal to $320. This is what you spend everyday. Times six days a week, equals $1920. Times four weeks in a month equals $7680.

Lets do the math, you have four children, your habit is $7680. a month. If you gave each one of your children $1000. for uniforms, tennis shoes and other school supplies. If you subtract your children $4000. from your crack money, you would still have $3680. left to blow up in crack smoke.

Take care of your children before your drug habit.

A Generational Curse
Who is watching you

Before you hit that woman, remember your children are watching. Sometimes that gives birth to a generational curse. You ask, "How can that be?"

You watched your father slap your mother, you slap your wife, and your son watched you and has begun to fight his wife. Now you have three generations of fighters.

I often wonder if a **wife beater** would defend his mother or sister if someone was beating one of them.
How about your daughter? Or would you tell your daughter to "behave" so she does not get hit.

Somewhere the "beating" has to stop. If you are the person where the generational curse can cease them **STOP** the curse. Do it right now! You can raise your family with **LOVE** and not with an **IRON fist.**

Young Ladies

Are we having fun...Yet?

Some of you have killed people to get money for drugs. Only to go to jail for life.
Are you having fun yet?

Others are robbing banks and other businesses, they get no money and they go straight "pass go" to jail. The bank robbery failed because the blue dye exploded in their face when they opened the bank bag.
Are you having fun yet?

Do you know anyone who robbed a bank, a grocery store, a bar and got enough cash, to buy a home, a new car and live happily ever after?
Never having any money problems again. Did they retire after the robbery? With good health insurance.
A strong possibility the answer is NO!

Yet there are hundreds of thousands of you, across the United States, in jail, you never get rich, because that life style is only temporary.
It is the jail time that is eternal. You lose family, friends and your freedom.

Are you having fun...YET!

Babies... having babies

Part of the problem with untrained children, is untrained parents. We call it babies having babies. If a girl gets pregnant and drops out of school, she has not learned the basics, that come in grades K-12th

When a young girl has a baby, she treats the baby like a doll. If its a girl, she over dresses her, "to many ribbons" combs her hair until the baby falls asleep. If it is a boy, she buys him name brand cloths and expensive tennis shoes. Some go as far as getting one of his ears pierced, to look like the rappers on TV.

When a young lady drops out of elementary or middle school, she is nothing but a baby herself. Also, the baby's young father has probably moved on, looking for the next victim to impregnate. This cycle goes on from one generation to the next. You have the Power to change.

Wake Up!

Building your reputation in the hood

- You wanted everyone to fear you
- You started out as a bully
- With small crimes, such as: destroying others property, simple battery, skipping school, very negative and very angry.
- Your scare tactics are working, the neighborhood children are afraid of you. They avoid coming into contact with you because they do not want to fight.
- While you are building your "rep" in the hood, you are in and out of juvenile hall because you are too young to go to the adult jail. Your parents are upset and their heart breaking.
- You are at the age of twenty-one and have elevated to a harder form of criminal activity.
- You need to commit murder or arm robbery to wear that famous **ORANGE** jumpsuit, to get that respect in jail.
- Your criminal career has flourished now to have you sentenced to twenty-one years in prison.

You have accomplished your goals.
Do you remember the young people you use to terrorize? They are very happy you are in jail. Your parents are hurt, but they know where you are. You probably did not think about it, but now you have to fight to maintain your "rep" in jail. The people from neighborhood have forgotten about you. Now! Your rep does not matter to them.

Shame on you, little **GIRL**, you should have given your parents a grand child instead of a REP.

Self Esteem
Where is yours

When did you lose your self esteem? Where is your pride? It must be hard for you to look at yourself in the mirror.

Do you remember the days when your mother nurtured you in grade school, how she fought away the bullies when you were to young to fight for yourself? How she taught you to say **NO** when the boys tried to get under your skirt? Do you remember when they broke your heart and she was there to wipe the tears away and tell you, this to shall pass?

Well, here you are, a young college woman nineteen years old, living in an apartment and driving the car your parents are paying for. But, you have allowed a young man to move in with you to use your apartment, your car and your body without the benefit of marriage.

Add this to the list, you are buying the gas, and he is riding around all day in the car your parents are paying for.

Your parents ask you about the young man and you say, "Stay out of my business!" Why would you take that attitude with them? Your parents want the best for you.

A note of thought:
I wonder what your boyfriend wants for you. Would he still be with you without the free room and board, free food, and the free rides. The car and you.

To the Bully
My humble opinion

The "bully" has been around forever. He or she just change faces, it is the same <u>spirit.</u> You will find them in schools grades K-12th and college, too.

A spouse can be a bully. An employer can be a bully, etc. Now, bulling has found its way to the internet by way of "Cyber Bulling."

A bully is someone who uses their influence to threaten or frighten someone in order to get what they want. They have to put someone down to make themselves look or feel good.

To the person who is getting Bullied.

It is a good idea to keep a record of the incident. If you are a child inform someone who is in authority. If someone is there when the bulling happens, get their names.

Whenever the incident happens in school, immediately notify your principal. Keep a record of the incident, get copies, and if possible, get your principal to sign a copy. Tell your parents what, when and where the bulling happened.

If the incident is elevated to the law getting involved, your records of the incident would be helpful.

A Message to a Bully

Bully, have you ever wondered how it would feel to be bullied? Do you have family members, a mother, grandmother, daughter, son that has or is being bullied? What would you do? Would you be willing to come to their rescue? Would you fight for them, to show them that you mean business about your family members.

I am sure your answer is YES!
Well keep your hands and mouth off, others peoples family.
Remember...Do unto others as you would have them do unto you.

Respect
Killer

Shame on you!
Someone murdered a seventy year old man, who was checking on his property.

God people, what is wrong with some of you? Have you ever heard of the Ten Commandments. It is found in Exodus chapter 20 verse 13. It reads as follow. **"Thou Shall Not Kill."** That old man was not hurting anyone, and was attending to his own business.

Where is the respect for elders? If you keep waking up in the mornings you to will become an elder. Have we become so harden in our heart? Why is there no fear when hurting or killing any individual? Would you feel comfortable if someone hurt your grandparents or great grand parents?

People, please, please stop killing each other, bring back "respect" for others and yourself.

IT BEGINS WITH YOU.

Signs of the time
Posting dead people pictures

How could you?

What kind of person takes a picture of a person who has died in a car accident. They do not stop there, they post the accident and picture of the deceased on the internet. Have some of us become so **cold** to the consideration and feelings of others?

Is this a new trend? Did their children see them with missing limbs on the net. Do you think that your mother would enjoy seeing you in that condition?

Get a Life! Stop sensationalizing things at other peoples expense.

Let us try to be more empathetic.

Revenge
Sick young man

Recently, I saw the picture of a handsome, young man who has a nice apartment and a beautiful black Jaguar automobile.

He says the car helps him to attract the young women. It does not matter, to him, what the young women look like because he only wants sex. He says he prefers heavy or fat women because, many of them have low self-esteem. His good looks and passion make the heavy girls think they won the lottery.

After the sex they thinks he will start a relationship with them. **NOT.** He has lost count of how many young women he has had sex with. Why so "highly" sexual?

The young handsome man is very bitter and angry because a pretty young woman gave him A I D S. Now his mission is to "infect" as many women as possible, he said, "I know I am going to die and I plan to take as many women with me as I can.

BEWARE
Revenge is mine saith the LORD

Happy New Year!

The definition of a new year's resolution is for a person to make a decision on the first day of the year; about the things that he/she intend to do or stop doing during that year.

The Vision

It would be nice if the crooks were tired of killing, raping and robbing. They all decided to turn over a new lease on life.
What if all the young men from ten years old to forty would not robbing, raping or killing? But, their new years resolution would be to go to school and not join a gang.

The young women from ten to forty years old would decide not to hit the night clubs, dropping it like its hot. They would stay home and teach their children manners and how to solve conflict without using violence. Instead of looking in that man's face 24-7 she would be giving her children her undivided attention.

I see older adults with businesses taking young men under their wings and teaching them the skills to help them get employment.

Remember, In the vision, I see no one selling drugs and no one buying drugs. The people who are addicted, the law and others will help them get to a rehab facility. The children are elated because daddy is home and reading a bedtime story. The girls have daddy's love and attention.

They do not have to look for love in all the wrong places, especially in a Pimp.
But of course, this is just a "dream" of mine. It is not happening. I am a writer and I have a tendency to fantasize and to see things as I wish they were.

There is a verse in the bible that says, "Without a vision the people parish" Maybe, if others caught on to this vision, it could become a reality.

What was this child's mother doing that caused him to deny that she is his mom.

No! that is not my mom
No, man you must have been mistaken

My mom would not disgrace herself like that
Nor would she embarrass us like that.

I tried to play it off
No need to say anymore

Afterward

Someone told me that this book would not change the world. I never expected it to change the world.
THAT'S GODS BUSINESS

My prayer is that someone will see their life style here on these pages, and try to change. Or some mother would decide to put her children best interest first instead of her pleasures.

Or that young man would read this book and decide to work at the fast food place, instead of robbing it.

Not the end... The Beginning

About the Author

Earline was born in New Orleans, Louisiana. She is the mother of two sons and two adoptive daughters. She has always had a love and desire to help children. This inspired Earline to be an active "Foster" parent for twenty years.

Earline Carr is a woman who greatly desires to fulfill and to show the love of Jesus Christ fully activated in her life. Her compassion for people is what motivated her to write. She saw there was a need for these words of "truth" to help people to become liberated from the "spirit" of self destruction.

The eyes of the Lord are in every place, beholding the evil and the good
Proverbs chapter-15 verse-3

The fear of the Lord prolongeth days: but the years of the wicked shall be shortened.
Proverbs chapter-10 verse-27

Honor thy Father and thy Mother

www.ingramcontent.com/pod-product-compliance
Lightning Source LLC
Chambersburg PA
CBHW042010150426
43195CB00002B/77